1000 tir

The Milleni

Jesus

Andrew Barker

Cover picture: .
Scripture quotations are from the New King James
Version
Published April 2021
ISBN:

Contents

Preface

"Better is one day in your courts, than a thousand elsewhere"

The Millenium is without doubt one of the most "out there" teachings of the Bible. The virgin birth, the parting of the red sea, and the resurrection of Jesus are all supernatural events, but I guess they have, at least in the church, become the accepted building blocks on which we base our faith. And it is easier to accept these pillars of our faith because they are history. But what is truly amazing, and hard to comprehend, is that the baby born in a manger, who never sought an earthly kingdom, but was crucified by His enemies, is prophesied to come back in the future to rule over Israel and the whole Earth for one thousand years.

So hard to comprehend, in fact, that in 30 years I have never heard a message given in church about the Millenium. The Millenium raises such a lot of questions and concerns, that I understand the desire not to go there. The evidence for the Millenium is patched together from many different old and new testament books, it is not given simply all in one easy to read passage. So we will be going on a journey. A journey where we unveil scriptures and ask ourselves: "if this is not referring to the Millenium, what on earth is it talking about?". I hope that by the end of the book, you will find an excitement growing, as you understand that God has a great plan for the future, yes it will get a lot worse before it gets better, but the future is peace like you have never known.

Obvoiusly the main concern is that end times teaching is sometimes the focus of fringe church organizations, not to mention the cults that have become infamous for their obesession with end time teaching. I am thinking in particular of the 1993 Waco cult led by David Koresh, and Heaven's Gate famous for the 1997 mass suicide. So naturally we shy away from anything that hints of such madness. The only thing which has brought me back to end times teaching, is that the Bible has plenty to say about it, and Jesus gave detailed account of it.

So the responses to my interest in the Millenium have been totally understandable. For instance – "I have always made the decision to live in the now, why should we fill our minds with the future?" I totally get that view. In fact Jesus said the same: "Do not worry about tomorrow, for tomorrow will worry about its own things. Sufficient for the day is its own trouble". But I always find that I worry less if I know what is coming. It is uncertainty that breeds anxiety. And maybe for that reason, when the disciples asked Jesus in Matthew 24 "what will be the sign of your coming, and of the end of the world", Jesus did not reply by saying "Look guys, the end of the world is well in the future, all you need to focus on is doing my will in the here and now". No ... quite amazingly, Jesus proceeded to launch into a message which gave quite a bit of detail about the end times. Even though, for them, it really was well in the future.

Two interesting things to note about Jesus's response to this question: He began by saying "Take heed that no one deceives you". Deception can only work on the minds of those who are unaware of the truth. So, especially if the end times are near, I think it is a very wise move to understand the prophecies of the Bible so that we are protected from deception.

The second thing is the illustration that Jesus gave at the end of this discourse. He compared His return to Noah's flood. People were focused on enjoying their lives until the day that Noah entered the ark. They knew nothing of the impending disaster until the flood washed them away. Evidently for a large part of the population there was no idea that the end was nigh. And in the same way, Jesus says that the world in this day and hour will similarly have no idea how near we are to the end. In verse 43-44 Jesus says something interesting: " But know this, that if the master of the house had known what hour the thief would come, he would have watched and not allowed his house to be broken into. **44** Therefore you also be ready, for the Son of Man is coming at an hour you do not expect."

This implies that although we do not know the

precise time Jesus will return, His advice to us is to be ready. Being ready actually communicates that we do not know exactly when something will happen, but it implies that we understand the season that we are in, and live in such a way to be prepared for a particular event. Where we may have become dulled or careless, we need to wake up and prioritize our lives according to the season that we perceive to be in.

Another more concerned view, when I shared my new found interest in the Millenium was this: Bible scholars have been interpreting the prophetic scriptures for many hundreds of years, and do so from a very learned viewpoint, taking great care to carefully differentiate between scripture that is poetic and symbolic, and scripture that can be taken literally. I might be seen as a crazy upstart if I begin claiming that symbolic scripture can be taken literally. To make matters worse I have no theological education. I take this advice very seriously, because I understand the importance of taking a balanced and informed understanding of scripture, not trying to make it arrive at conclusions that I have pre-determined. I guess that by the time you reach the end of this book, you will either get that inner nudge that I am indeed another crackpot end times fanatic, or, if I have not based this book on my own wild assumptions, you will hopefully feel the peace of God which comes from digging into truth.

The funniest line came from my daughter "Dad i think

you should lay off the books ... try not to go crazy in this lockdown". So I get it, some are going stir crazy, some are burying themselves in hobbies, and here I am studying about the Millenium to the point of obsession. And i totally accept that a lot of end times teachers don't talk about anything else, so that to all the world they really seem to have lost the plot. Or, have they found the plot, but are so excited that they forget to integrate the end times plot with the rest of the bible, and with day to day life?

To summarize my introduction, I want to assure you that I am not going to make predictions about the Millenium based on my own assumptions. But I am going to unpack scriptures to show that the Millenium is a soon coming reality. I am also going to unpack some detail of life in the Millenium.

Finally I want to say that the reason for this study is to remove the anxiety or bewilderment one might feel as this new age approaches. I want to show more than anything that the Millenium will be the closest thing to Heaven on Earth. If that is really true, then my aim is to stir up such a hope and a joy, that "for the joy set before you" you will be able to endure the Tribulation Period that directly preceeds it. My purpose is also to develop our eternal mindset. How difficult we find it to let go of our dreams, our possessions and ultimately our lives. But surely, it is our eternal hope which enables us to "lose our lives for His sake", that we may really find our lives. And although the ultimate destiny is the eternal Jerusalem in that new Earth and Heaven, I am going to prove that the Millenium is where we will next find ourselves, if we stand up for Jesus.

1 – A, post or Pre (say what?)

The first thing I need to do is to explain that there are three main theological interpretations of the Millenium: Amillennialism, Postmillennialism and Premillennialism. Here are brief summaries of each viewpoint:

Amillennialism

This view is so named to convey that there is not a literal Millenium. Amilleniallists take a very liberal view of the book of Revelation and other end time prophecies. The general understanding is that these prophecies are a symbolic and poetic picture of God's triumph over evil. This view does not believe in a physical rule of Jesus as King of Israel and the Earth. Amillennialists either (like the postmillennialist) see the church age as the spiritual reign of Jesus in the hearts of believers on Earth, or they interpret the Millenium as the heavenly reign of Jesus over the saints in heaven. Either way, the amillennialist view dismisses a literal timescale of one thousand years.

Some amillennialists expect a future Tribulation Period caused by the release of satan from the abyss in which he is supposedly currently bound, but they believe that the account of the Tribulation Period (seals, trumpets and bowls) in the book of Revelation can only be taken very loosely and symbolically. In general you will find that the view of the high (very traditional) church is amillennialist.

The problem with the amillennialist view is that there are so many prophecies concerning Israel and the return of Jesus in the last days which have to be ignored in the process. This view encourages symbolic interpretation of scripture so that it is then difficult to assess what should be taken literally. Surely this can only result in confusion surrounding scriptural interpretation, and a diminished, if not a completely redundant view of biblical prophecy concerning Israel. To me, amillennialism is not so much an error, as it is simply a distinterest in biblical prophecy, and a disinterest in any hope of a future earthly kingdom.

Postmillennialism

This view is so named to convey that Jesus's second coming will occur after the Millenium period, which some hold to mean a literal thousand years. Therefore postmillennialists believe that we are already in the Millenium, which began sometime in the past, and will end sometime in the future with the rapture. Jesus is on his spiritual throne in heaven, and reigning through the church, as they gradually evangelize the whole world. This view arose in the 19th century and is now taken by a variety of evangelical churches.

Many postmillennialists are also "full preterists", in

other words they believe that much of the tribulation prophecies in the book of Revelation and Daniel were fulfilled in the destruction of Jerusalem in AD70. Full preterists believe that the Roman emperor Nero was the antichrist.

The problems with postmillennialism are many: If the church age does not culminate with the eventual conversion of most of the world, but instead culminates in the Tribulation Period, those who have adopted this view will be confused and disheartened when the Tribulation Period arrives. In fact it could be true to say that the Tribulation Period will catch postmillennialists unawares, the very thing that Jesus warned of in Matthew 24. I would put this as the most dangerous aspect of the postmillenniallist view.

The postmillennialist view teaches that satan is currently bound, since Revelation teaches that at the beginning of the Millenium, satan is bound and thrown into an abyss. It is very difficult to understand how this view can be taken seriously, since evil of every kind has only become more prevalent in the last two thousand years.

A postmillennialist church which is focussed on expansion, evangelizing and progress (while these are admirable aims) can find that leaders are tempted to focus on success, programs for church growth and such like. It is simply an inbuilt desire of the human race to achieve. Such a church can become man-centred, and can tend to follow man-made programs, rather than simple reliance on God. Like amillennialism, postmillennialism has no place for the fullfilment of prophecy concerning Israel, and has to symbolize and spiritualize a lot of prophecy concerning the physical earthly reign of Jesus.

This is the next dangerous side to postmillennialism: One has to believe that God will break His promises to Israel (and there are many yet unfulfilled), or maybe the promises cannot be taken literally, or maybe God is not infinitely loyal. When God says "Can a mother forget the baby at her breast and have no compassion on the child she has borne? Though she may forget, I will not forget you" are we to take this as a romantic notion that has faded into history? Surely if we take this view, we are ranking God with every other absentee father who has walked away from his family. You might think that so much time has passed since Israel had a heart for God, that He has moved on. Not so! God has an infinitely long memory. The words He spoke to Abraham, Jacob, Moses, Joshua, David and others seem like only yesterday to Him.

To me, where amillennialists are simply sticking their heads in the sand (and therefore not likely to attract too much following) the opposite is true of postmillennialists. Postmillennialists have built a teaching which has signposts to prophetic fullfilments poining in the wrong direction. Time will tell, but i think that postmillennialism will become unstuck in the future.

Premillennialism

I will not hide the fact that this book is built purely on the premillennialist view. This view holds that the second coming of Jesus directly preceeds the Millenium. The great tribulation in turn directly preceeds Jesus's return. This view enables you to take biblical prophecy literally, and although we therefore will face a time of tribulation like the world has never seen, we also have an amazing hope: The earthly physical thousand year reign of Jesus as King over Israel and the Earth.

This view was the only view of the early church, it was the main view of the church until the 19th century, and is now a popular view in many evangelical churches worldwide.

Objections:

Objectors believe that biblical prophecy is a subject to be handled only by those who are theologically trained to understand hermeneutics, or how to interpret biblical texts: basically to know when to take a text symbolically, and when to take a text literally. So, objectors hold that only the untrained would take an extensively literal view of scripture, and therefore the premillennial view should not be trusted, as its source is not from trained theologians.

However to counter this, I have found premillennialism to be the most honest view, it does not ignore parts of the bible to fit its teaching, it encourages as much literal interpretation of the bible as possible, it looks to the fullfilment of all the unfulfilled prophecies regarding Israel, and it makes a lot more sense of scriptures which talk about Jesus ruling from the throne of David.

There is no doubt that premillennialism could be considered too fantastic an idea, the thought that Jesus would live among us again.... However He lived among us 2000 years ago, why should He not live among us again? Although this time not as a lamb or a suffering servant, but as a lion, as the King of kings.

Finally, no one wants to believe that we are headed for a great tribulation. When you read the vision of John in the book of Revelation, one word describes this period, it is pure horror from a natural viewpoint, but with an eternal perspective Jesus said we would endure. If indeed this period is approaching, I would rather know in advance than be caught out. I would rather stand strong in faith than be deceived or offended. I would rather read a bible i can trust literally, than one that needs complex interpretation. The premillennialist is definitely not preterist: The Tribulation Period is in the future.

2 - A brief look back

Although this study is of the Millenium period, it has to start with the outcome of the Tribulation Period, so we need to look at this period carefully. It is important that we do not over-exaggerate the events of the Tribulation, but also important that we do not overlook the details revealed in the book of Revelation.

The tribulation is a short period in which the Antichrist will rise to power and conquer many nations. Beginning with the appearance of the Antichrist there are 7 seals opened which herald war, killing, economic disaster, famine and disease. These events will be mostly the outcome of the Antichrist's warfare and aggression. Revelation 6 vs 8 shows that a quarter of the World will die in this time. If we take the bible literally, that equates to 2 billion lives. This leaves 6 billion people alive.

Following this there will be 7 trumpets which will herald events which could be summarized mainly as natural and cosmic disasters. Revelation chapter 8 describes events such as collisions with NEOs (Near Earth Objects), a huge volcanic explosion which throws a whole mountain into the sea, and a huge army of two hundred million who kill a third of mankind. If we take the bible literally, that is another 2 billion lives killed. This leaves 4 billion alive on Earth. This is a best case scenario, as surely the cosmic and natural disasters will affect many, but no mention of figures is made relating to these, save the 7000 killed in the earthquake heralded by the seventh trumpet.

Finally there are 7 bowl judgements, and unlike the seals and trumpets, these bowls are actually described as the wrath of God. These events will bring not death, but torture, pain, thirst (all water will be turned to blood), extreme solar heat and darkness. The last bowl causes the greatest earthquake ever known to man, so that all cities fall into rubble, and huge lethal hailstones will fall out of the sky. Then follows the battle of Armageddon in which all the armies of the Antichrist are killed by the sword coming from the mouth of Jesus. We can understand this sword to be the Word of God (often described in the Bible as the Sword of the Spirit), which has the power to create life or take it.

There are no exact figures given here, but a quick google search will tell you that in the coming decades, up to 70% of the world population will be living in cities, and would mostly be killed in such an earthquake as described in Revelation 16. Realistically then, the best case scenario is that there will be 1 billion people left alive on Earth at the end of the Tribulation Period. This does not account for the armies of the Antichrist who die in the Battle of Armageddon. If the Antichrist's armies are one and the same as the army of 200 million, then it takes the surviving population figure down to around 800 million.

While it is foolish to make calculations like this as a basis for predicting the exact final outome of the Tribulation Period, I think it is right to understand the gravity of the situation, and to realize that according to the scant figures given in the book of Revelation, the population of Earth will be well and truly decimated in the Tribulation Period.

You might ask why such an analysis is necessary. Surely it would be better not to know this? I disagree. If this knowledge pushes you to start living with an eternal perspective then I have done my job. If this knowledge shows you how fragile life on Earth is, and how important it is to make Heaven your home, then I have done my job. If this knowledge causes you to reprioritise your life to win souls, then I have done my job.

Why else should we be aware of the destruction which the Tribulation Period will bring? I believe it will help us understand more of what the Millenium will be like. I have read some books on the Millenium which almost ignore that the whole world has been decimated and turned to rubble. And so they just assume that everything will carry on as normal from where they briefly left off. I would find this hard to believe, given the story that unfolds in the book of Revelation.

Also, given the absolute horrors of the Tribulation Period, it is hard to believe that the remaining human race will pursue the same ideas and beliefs that they do now. You often hear that people who survive a near death experience are changed forever. They re-prioritize their lives, they leave behind meaningless pursuits, they make time for what is really significant, they often devote their lives to charitable work, they are a humbled people, who know that "there but for the grace of God go I".

So I want you to dream for a bit. You have just survived the most unbelievable 3 years of your life, having escaped death a number of times, and seen disasters too horrendous to describe. If you are a war veteran, forgive me, but the Bible plainly says that the Tribulation Period will far outweigh anything you have seen. And yet you and your family have survived, and you find that Jesus is now King of Israel, and we are living in a new age, you would almost call it a new civilisation.

Are you honestly at this point yearning to see a comedian make fun of the whole thing ... or perhaps you might want to get back to playing computer games 6 hours a day .... Surely you are desparate to go to a premiership football match ... oh, wait, the team died during the Tribulation Period, actually so have all the other teams .... maybe you used to be an art collector, do you fancy buying another expensive item?.. When you next visit a restaurant will you complain if the food is not to your liking? Or maybe you would like to travel to see the world – If you like demolition sites – well ok, if that is not an option, maybe we could all go on holiday to the beach, but the last time we tried that we were nearly all killed by a massive tsunami.

I apologize for being brutal. What I am trying to impress on you is this: After the Tribulation Period, i cannot see mankind easily transitioning back to the plethora of vain pursuits that fill our lives today. Surely our hearts will be so deeply humbled that vain pursuits (these are not even sins) will appear repulsive and utterly selfish. Surely our only ambition will be to help others, to understand why the Tribulation Period had to happen, and get to know the God who has allowed us to survive, and whose son sits on the Throne of David.

With this in mind we can more readily understand what life will be like in the Millenium. There are scriptures which give detail about what Jesus's earthly reign will accomplish, and the different aspects of His kingdom, and life in that kingdom.

Also, with this background in mind, I have added one chapter which relays my personal view on how the new civilisation will work, in comparison with how civilisation works now. I must emphasize that this final chapter is not evidenced by scripture, instead I have tried to imagine how the new kingdom would

mirror the heart of God in terms of the factors that
will characterize this new civilisation.

3 – When will the Millenium begin?

I am hoping that this is the chapter that will wake you up out of your slumber. This is where we change gears...Because if the end times and the Millenium are hundreds of years away, then of what interest are they to us now? Yes, there could be some casual interest for the thorough student of scripture. But, a bit like a road journey from London to Edinborough to visit your long lost aunty, you don't need the sat nav on until you get near the destination. And so we don't need this focus on the Millenium unless we are close. And so my job here is to investigate how near we are to the end.

Pointers to the season we are in

Earlier I gave a brief summary of the disasters to befall mankind in the Tribulation Period. Now I want to look at a very quick summary of the antichrist's end time mission. He will conquer nations, he will invade Israel, he will ransack Jerusalem, he will abolish the jewish temple sacrifices, and occupy the jewish temple, claiming to be God. This prophecy was written by Daniel around 500BC, and confirmed by Jesus in Matthew 24. So it was first unveiled over 2500 years ago. Then in AD70, Jerusalem was destroyed by the Romans, and the nation of Israel was no more.

Roughly two millenia later in 1917, the Balfour

Declaration requested a homeland for the jews. Zionism grew for many reasons during the first world war, for example it was thought that the jews in the Russian Bolshevic party would be more willing to assist the allied war efforts if they were promised the reward of a jewish state.

At the same time the allies were fighting the Ottoman Empire (Turkey) with the help of the arab nationalists, who were also promised the land of Palestine, but when the war was over, the Post war Sykes-Picot agreement divided up the Middle East between France and Great Britain. The arab leader Faisal I bin Al-Hussein was let down by this agreement which did not give him the pan-arab kingdom he had hoped for. However Faisal was eventually made king of Iraq.

The British were responsible for the land of Palestine east of the Jordan, and facilitated the return of jews to the land in which their ancestors had once lived. Understandably the arabs of Palestine saw this as a colonial move, and resisted the increasing arrival of jews. This led to conflict between the British colonialists and the arab population, and by 1947 this contentious issue was given to the United Nations to solve, who divided up this land to create a jewish and Palestinian state.

However the Palestinians did not accept their lot and the surrounding nations declared war on Israel in 1948, but by a miracle Israel won this war and expanded her borders. Various agreements have since been made to give land back to Palestinians, but palestinian terrorist groups have ignored the agreements made at a political level, and sought to destroy the nation of Israel. However messy the process has been, it has nevertheless resulted in a modern day Israel, without which the prophecies of Daniel could not come to pass.

So I get the feeling that in terms of the long journey from Daniel to the end times, God switched on the sat nav in 1948. However this is not the only significant date. In 1967 the nation of Israel took back the old city of East Jerusalem from the arab nations. Again, unless Israel occupy the old city, and build a jewish temple, the antichrist cannot fulfill end time prophecy. So in a ball park sense, we have been near the end times since 1967.

But can we get more accurate detail? I think so: In Matthew 24 vs 32-34, at the end of Jesus's teaching about the end times, He says

32 "Now learn this parable from the fig tree: When its branch has already become tender and puts forth leaves, you know that summer *is* near. **33** So you also, when you see all these things, know that it is near—at the doors! **34** Assuredly, I say to you, this generation will by no means pass away till all these things take place.

Firstly, what does the fig tree represent? It is accepted that the fig tree is a metaphor for Israel. In the winter, trees look dead. And certainly Israel looked dead until 1948. I would compare the re-instatement of Israel to the budding, or coming back to life of the fig tree.

Then Jesus says: So you also, when you see all these things, know that it is near – this generation wil not pass away till all these things take place.

We know that Jesus was not referring to the generation of the disciples, for they are now all dead. So who was Jesus referring to? Could it be that in God's wisdom, He knew that this scripture would be not only heard by the disciples, but also read by you and me. So not only were these words for the disciples, but for us also. And when we see the budding of Israel, could it be that our generation will not pass away until all these things take place?

If this is so, then how long does it take for a generation to pass away? Anything up to 120 years, by all accounts, but more likely around 70-80 years. Does this mean that the generation born in 1948 will see the end times before they pass away, ie anytime from now until around 2070?

It is wrong to pinpoint a date or a year to the end times, but I believe that it is right to be aware of the season, and I think that 50 years is a respectable season. Jesus said that no one knows the day or the hour of His return. However this same Jesus said in Luke 21 vs 34-36:

34 "But take heed to yourselves, lest your hearts be weighed down with carousing, drunkenness, and cares of this life, and that Day come on you unexpectedly. **35** For it will come as a snare on all those who dwell on the face of the whole earth. **36** Watch therefore, and pray always that you may be counted worthy to escape all these things that will come to pass, and to stand before the Son of Man."

In other words, do not let the end times arrive unexpectedly. For those who are weighed down with cares and occupied with partying, that day will come as a trap. For those who watch and pray, it will be a day to escape, not be trapped. But if you are not aware of the season, surely the temptation is to go to sleep spiritually.

A similar message can be found in 1 Thessalonians chapter 5: "**2** For you yourselves know perfectly that the day of the Lord so comes as a thief in the night. **3** For when they say, "Peace and safety!" then sudden destruction comes upon them, as labor pains upon a pregnant woman. And they shall not escape. **4** But you, brethren, are not in darkness, so that this Day should overtake you as a thief."

In other words, we are supposed to be aware of the

season. We should not be afraid of being labelled as weird or heretical when we point to the season of Jesus's return. Those who are aware of this season will have a greater fear of the Lord, and a greater desire to win souls. Those who are unaware of the season? They will be busy buying and selling, marrying and partying. Not that these are particularly sins, but the message from Jesus is that we should not be too busy to prepare for His return. If we are in this category of "too busy", the day of the Lord will come as sudden destruction. As the day approaches this should create a desire to walk closely to God.

Length of the Tribulation Period

The book of Revelation teaches that the first sign of the end times will be the appearance of the antichrist. Following that, the Tribulation Period begins. What is not so clear is how long this period will last. Traditional eschatology teaches that Daniel's prophecy in chapter 9 shows that the antichrist will establish a covenant with many (not necessarily meaning Israel) for one week, but this is taken to mean 7 years. In the middle of this period he will invade Israel, occupy the temple and stop the jewish sacrifices.

"And he [Antichrist] shall confirm the covenant with many for one week: and in the midst of the week he shall cause the sacrifice and the oblation to cease, and for the overspreading of abominations he shall make it desolate, even until the consummation, and that determined shall be poured upon the desolate." (Daniel 9:27)

But in many other places it says that the antichrist will have power for 42 months or three and a half years:

1. Gentiles shall trample the Holy City for 42 months (Rev 11 vs 2)
2. Half of Jerusalem flees from the antichrist armies to the wilderness, where God sustains her for 1260 days (Rev 12 vs 6)
3. Again, it mentions that Israel is hidden from the serpent in the desert for a time, times and half a time (3.5 years) (Rev 12 vs 14)
4. Power is given to the beast of Revelation to continue for 42 months (Rev 13 vs 5)
5. Daniel 7 vs25 says that the saints and times will be given into his hands for a time, and times and half a time (3.5 years)
6. Daniel 12 vs 11 also says that 1290 days shall pass since the temple sacrifices are removed and the abomination that causes desolation is set up.

Two conclusions:

The Tribulation Period is actually only 3.5 years long. In this case the antichrist will invade Israel at the beginning of his rule.
Or

The Tribulation Period is 7 years long, in the first 3.5 years, the antichrist will set up his empire and conquer other nations. In the middle of this period he will turn his attention on Israel, invade and occupy the temple.

Length of the Millenium period

The Millenium will begin directly after the battle of Armageddon, which takes place at the end of the Tribulation Period. The earthly rule of Jesus is referred to throughout the Old Testament, but it is only in the book of Revelation that we see how long this rule will last. Revelation 20 vs 4 says:

4 And I saw thrones, and they sat on them, and judgment was committed to them. Then *I saw* the souls of those who had been beheaded for their witness to Jesus and for the word of God, who had not worshiped the beast or his image, and had not received *his* mark on their foreheads or on their hands. And they lived and reigned with Christ for **a thousand years**.

So, to summarize: The fig tree parable tells us that we should expect the end times any time from now to around mid century. The awesome reality is that the Millenium can be expected to begin equally soon, seeing that only a handful of years (the tribulation) separate this current age from the Millenium Kingdom.

4 – Why must there be a Millenium?

Now that I have woken you up, I want to prove that this is no false alarm. I want to show from many parts of the Bible that the physical earthly rule of Jesus and the rise of Israel are yet unfulfilled prophecies. When you link this up with the Book of Revelation, it points very definitely to a Millenium Kingdom.

Numbers 24: We start getting hints towards an all powerful Israelite kingdom in Balaam's prophecy in Numbers 24 vs 17 "I see Him, but not now; I behold Him, but not near; A star shall come forth from Jacob, and a sceptre shall rise from Israel..." Balaam then talks about this ruler crushing and tearing down and possessing all the enemies of Israel. Now, although Israel won many wars after this prophecy, they were not the dominating force in the land. No sooner had they defeated one country, they were under attack from another. Israel had many kings. But this prophecy talks of a star (heavenly being of light) coming from the descendants of Jacob. He will not just be any king. He will not only rule Israel, but also the enemies of Israel. So great will be his rule, that he will be known as a sceptre. Balaam also infers that he is seeing well into the future. This picture perfectly describes an earthly reign of Jesus, the Son of God.

1 Chronicles 17: This earthly reign of Jesus is also implied in Nathan's prophecy to King David in 1 Chronicles 17 vs 11-14.

¹¹ And it shall be, when your days are fulfilled, when you must go *to be* with your fathers, that I will set up your seed after you, who will be of your sons; and I will establish his kingdom. ¹² He shall build Me a house, and I will establish his throne forever. ¹³ I will be his Father, and he shall be My son; and I will not take My mercy away from him, as I took *it* from *him* who was before you. ¹⁴ And I will establish him in My house and in My kingdom forever; and his throne shall be established forever.

The prophecy is partially fulfilled by Solomon who does indeed build a temple. But His throne is not established forever. And Solomon is not established in God's house and in this kingdom forever. This prophecy leaves you thinking that maybe Nathan was simply getting over excited about David's successor, Solomon. But does God speak exaggerations through His prophets? I think that the way to understand this prophecy is to understand that it was partially fulfilled by Solomon, however it also seems to apply to a future son of David. This future son will build a house (temple) for God. His throne will be established forever. God's lovingkindness will not be removed from Him. He will be established in the temple and in the kingdom of Israel forever. There is no descendant of David who has qualified to fulfill this prophecy. None, that is, unless Jesus returns to rule Israel eternally.

David speaks prophetically in the psalms many times about a king who will reign over Israel forever. Apart from Jesus, who can these prophecies refer to?

Psalm 2 is labelled "The Messiah's Triumph and Kingdom". Evidently the translators can sense that this psalm points towards the Millenium.

It begins "Why do the nations rage, and the peoples plot a vain thing?"

There is no doubt that before the mIllenium arrives, the antichrist will stir up extreme rage against Israel. In Daniel chapter 8 vs 23 - 25 it describes the antichrist as cunning, and a master of deception. There is more detail in chapter 11: He shall obtain the kingdom by flattery, and verse 23: From the time that an alliance is made with him, he shall act deceitfully. Verse 27: Seeking nothing but each other's harm, these kings will plot against each other at the conference table, attempting to deceive each other.

God's answer? vs 6: Yet I have set my king on my holy hill of Zion

vesrse 7: The Lord has said to me: You are my Son, today i have begotten you. Ask of me and I will give you the nations for your inheritance, and the ends of the earth for your possession....

It continues in verse 10: Now therefore be wise, O kings; Be instructed, you judges of the earth. Serve the Lord with fear, and rejoice with trembling. Kiss the Son, lest He be angry ... Blessed are all those who put their trust in Him.

As you read this you cannot help but wonder: The king described in verse 6 ... is this the same as the Son of verse 7 .... is this the same as the Lord and Son of verse 10?

Matthew Henry says at the beginning of his commentary of psalm 2: "As the foregoing psalm was moral, and showed us our duty, so this is evangelical, and shows us our Saviour. Under the type of David's kingdom (which was of divine appointment, met with much opposition, but prevailed at last) the kingdom of the Messiah, the Son of David, is prophesied of, which is the primary intention and scope of the psalm; and I think there is less in it of the type, and more of the anti-type, than in any of the gospel psalms, for there is nothing in it but what is applicable to Christ, but some things that are not at all applicable to David. (v. 6, v. 7): "Thou art my Son" (v. 8), "I will give thee the uttermost parts of the earth," and (v. 12), "Kiss the Son." It is interpreted of Christ Acts. 4:24 Acts. 13:33 ; Heb. 1:5 . The Holy Ghost here foretels,
I. The opposition that should be given to the kingdom of the Messiah (v. 1-3).
II. The baffling and chastising of that opposition

(<u>v. 4</u>, v. 5).
III. The setting up of the kingdom of Christ, notwithstanding that opposition (<u>v. 6</u>).
IV. The confirmation and establishment of it (<u>v. 7</u>).
V. A promise of the enlargement and success of it (<u>v. 8</u>, v. 9).
VI. A call and exhortation to kings and princes to yield themselves the willing subjects of this kingdom, (<u>v. 10-12</u>)."

It is hard to conclude anything except that in this psalm, God is telling us of an earthly kingdom which extends throughout the earth, over which Jesus is King, whose throne is located in Israel.

Psalm 24 vs7-10: "Lift up your heads, O ye gates; and be lifted up, you everlasting doors; and the King of Glory shall come in. Who is this King of Glory? The Lord strong and mighty, the Lord mighty in battle. Lift up your heads, O ye gates; and be lifted up, you everlasting doors; and the King of Glory shall come in. Who is this King of Glory? The Lord of hosts, He is the King of Glory.

In psalm 24, the gates and doors are told to lift up their heads. Which gates and doors are these? Could they be the gates of Jerusalem? And no wonder they ask not once, but twice: "Who is this King?" When Jesus enters Jerusalem to begin His reign, well might you ask, "who is this king?". For it will be asked in hushed tones, it will be a question on the lips of astounded onlookers, it will be a very valid question, for never in all the history of the world has such a king been seen as Jesus.

The world has known him as a baby. They are familiar with the gospel accounts of his ministry in first century Israel. Most know of his crucifxion. Some believe in his resurrection. But very few have amy idea that He is returning to earth to rule as a king!

And even when they lay eyes on Him, they will ackowledge that this king is the most humble, yet the most powerful and fearless person they have ever seen, but still it will be the farthest thing from their wildest dreams that this king could be the baby born in the manger who was rejected by the world. And so they will ask ....

Psalm 46: My comments are added throughout this psalm. It points very clearly to the end times, and the Millenium kingdom.

God *is* our refuge and strength,
A very present help in trouble.
² Therefore we will not fear,
Even though the earth be removed,
And though the mountains be carried into the midst of the sea;
³ *Though* its waters roar *and* be troubled,
Though the mountains shake with its swelling. *Selah*

In Revelation 16 vs 20, at the pouring out of the seventh vial, there is an earthquake that is simply described as the greatest earthquake in history, resulting in "every island fleeing away, and the mountains not found". In Luke 21 vs 25 one depiction of the tribulation period includes "the sea and the waves roaring"

4 *There is* a river whose streams shall make glad the city of God,
The holy *place* of the ⌊tabernacle of the Most High.
5 God *is* in the midst of her, she shall not be moved;
God shall help her, just at the break of dawn.
6 The nations raged, the kingdoms were moved;
He uttered His voice, the earth melted.
7 The LORD of hosts *is* with us;
The God of Jacob *is* our refuge. *Selah*

As we covered in Psalm 2, the nations of the antichrist kingdom will rage against Israel, but God will help her at the last watch of night, at the break of dawn. This help will take the form of the return of Jesus, the Lord of hosts, he will defeat the antichrist armies with his word. He will utter his voice and the enemy will melt.

8 Come, behold the works of the LORD,
Who has made desolations in the earth.
9 He makes wars cease to the end of the earth;
He breaks the bow and cuts the spear in two;
He burns the chariot in the fire.
10 Be still, and know that I *am* God;

I will be exalted among the nations,
I will be exalted in the earth!
[11] The Lᴏʀᴅ of hosts *is* with us;
The God of Jacob *is* our refuge.

*Isaiah 2 vs 4 and Micah 4 vs 3 both prophesy of the
latter days, when Israel will be exalted above all other
nations, when people will say, "come let's go to the
house of the God of Jacob, He shall teach us His
ways", a time when the Lord will judge between
nations, and they will beat their swords into
ploughshares, and their spears into pruning hooks, a
time when nations shall not lift a sword against each
other anymore. This will be a time when Jesus truly is
exalted among all nations, for He will finally be with
us, as King of Israel, and king of the earth.*

Psalm 47: "For the Lord most high is a great king over
all the Earth, He will subdue the peoples under us,
and the nations under our feet. He will choose our
inheritance for us, the excellence of Jacob whom He
loves ... God reigns over the nations, God sits on His
holy throne. The princes of the people have
assembled themselves as the people of the God of
Abraham..."

Of this psalm, Matthew Henry says "Many suppose
that this psalm was penned upon occasion of the
bringing up of the ark to Mount Zion which seems to
refer to ("God has gone up with a shout");—but it
looks further, to the ascension of Christ into the

heavenly Zion, after he had finished his undertaking on earth, and to the setting up of his kingdom in the world, to which the heathen should become willing subjects."

I will add that when you take this psalm literally, it points to an earthly kingdom which begins with Israel, and extends over the entire earth, so that all rulers submit to Jesus as if they were themselves jews.

Isaiah 9 6-7:
"For unto us a Child is born,
Unto us a Son is given;
And the government will be upon His shoulder.
And His name will be called
Wonderful, Counselor, Mighty God,
Everlasting Father, Prince of Peace.
7 Of the increase of *His* government and peace
There will be no end,
Upon the throne of David and over His kingdom,
To order it and establish it with judgment and justice
From that time forward, even forever.
The zeal of the LORD of hosts will perform this."

This prophecy of Isaiah spells out that God's son will be given to us as a king. A king who will sit on David's throne and over his kingdom, to establish it forever. For Matthew Henry, this means that Jesus will reign over His church: *"God shall give him the throne of his father David,* Lu. 1:32, 33. The gospel church, in which Jew and Gentile are incorporated, is the holy hill of

Zion, on which Christ reigns"

For me, no clearer words can be found in the bible which tell us that Jesus is destined to reign over Israel. If you translate "the throne of David" as something other than the reign over the kingdom of Israel, i think you have to bend a lot of truth. I also think that people may go down these rabbit warrens because the thought of Jesus returning to rule physically over Israel is too amazing to comprehend, especially for those who are not particular supporters of Israel. But if you take it literally, then Isaiah literally meant that Jesus will be King over Israel! This did not happen the first time Jesus walked on earth, so it has to have a future fulfillment. Notice that no one is more excited about this than Jesus himself: The zeal of the Lord of hosts will perform this!

For me, the bottom line is that the Whole book of Isaiah is about God's dealings with Israel, and to make some of it refer to the church is in my opinion, a theologian's way of avoiding the subject of Christ's millenial rule.

Jeremiah 23 vs 5 says: Behold, the days come, saith the Lord, that I will raise unto David a righteous Branch, and a King shall reign and prosper, and shall execute judgment and justice in the earth.

Who is this righteous branch? Isaiah 11 talks about a shoot coming from the stump of Jesse. The Spirit of the Lord will rest on Him, the spirit of wisdom and understanding, counsel and might, the Spirit of knowledge and the fear of the Lord. And his delight will be in the fear of the Lord. He will not judge by what his eyes see, or decide disputes by what his ears hear. But with righteousness He will judge the poor, and decide with equity for the meek of the earth.

Who is this branch. Could it be David? Isaiah wrote this after the reign of David. I think we have to go on very complicated journies to arrive at any other conclusion than this: The righteous branch is Jesus. However Jeremiah calls him a king. A king who will reign and prosper, and execute justice in the earth. Currently it would be a stretch to say that Jesus is executing justice on the earth. However if Jeremiah 23 vs 5 describes the Millenium reign of Jesus as King over Israel and the earth, then it also follows that His earthly rule would affect everything on earth, including justice.

Jeremiah 30 vs 9 "But they shall serve the Lord their God, and David their King, whom I will raise up for them."

Sometimes there tends to be confusion over whether Jesus will be the future king of Israel, or whether David will be raised up to be the future king of Israel. There should not be confusion. With the return of Jesus, and with His dwelling place set to Be Zion, it makes no sense for a man (David) to be raised up to be king. Rather, when prophecies talk of David, I believe they are talking of his line, his ancestry, his descendant. I believe they are talking of Jesus.

Ezekiel continues in a similar vein in chapter 34 vs 23-24
I will establish one shepherd over them, and he shall feed them—My servant David. He shall feed them and be their shepherd. **24** And I, the LORD, will be their God, and My servant David a prince among them; I, the LORD, have spoken.

In the book of Joel (which most agree is written concerning the end times day of the Lord) we read in chapter 2: "Sound the trumpet in Jerusalem! Raise the alarm on my holy mountain! let everyone tremble in fear because the day of the Lord is upon us."

vs 10: "The sun and moon grow dark and the stars no longer shine .... the day of the Lord is an awesome terrible thing. Who can possibly survive?"

God then calls the armies of the nations to gather in the valley of Jehoshaphat. But they are gathered for one reason, and that is to face the wrath of God, a judgement for their attack on Israel. Thousands upon thousands are waiting in this valley. The valley of decision. Is it so named because the members of this army have one last chance to decide to decide against their false God, and turn to the real God? Or is it so named because this is the place where God's decision or judgement will be executed on them?

Which ever, chapter 3 verse 14 goes on to say: "There the day of the Lord will soon arrive. 15 The sun and moon will grow dark, and the stars will no longer shine. 16 The Lord's voice will roar from Zion and thunder from Jerusalem, and the heavens and earth will shake. But the Lord will be a refuge for his people, a strong fortress for the people of Israel. 17 So you shall know that I am the Lord your God, dwelling in Zion, my holy mountain. Jerusalem will be holy forever, and foreign armies will never conquer her again."

Finally verse 21 ends with "and I the Lord will make my home in Jerusalem with my people."

What are we to do with these scriptures? If these verses are indeed describing the battle of armageddon, then they also tell us that God will win this battle, and thereafter make Jerusalem His home.

Now let's look at prophecies about Jesus' Millenium reign from the New Testatment:

in Luke chapter 1 verses 26-33, the angel Gabriel said to Mary:
"....30 Do not be afraid, Mary, for you have found favor with God. **31** And behold, you will conceive in your womb and bring forth a Son, and shall call His name JESUS. **32** He will be great, and will be called the Son of the Highest; and the **Lord God will give Him**

the throne of His father David. 33 And He will reign over the house of Jacob forever, and of His kingdom there will be no end."

Then when the wise men arrive, they ask this question in Matthew 2 vs 2:
Where is he that is born King of the Jews? We read this verse every Christmas, but it must have been such an odd question at the time. Apart from Mary's personal message from Gabriel, no-one knew that Jesus was destined to be a King. Even Joseph was not told that Jesus would be a king. Saviour, yes, and Emmanuel, God with us, but no mention of taking the throne of David.

So apparently in those days, the only people who were informed of Jesus's destiny as a king were: Mary, the wise men, Herod and 33 years later, Pilate. When the baby Jesus was taken to the temple for circumcision, the prophets Simeon and Anna saw the baby and praised God for His salvation, believeing that Jesus was their Messiah, a light for the gentiles, and the glory of the people of Israel. But the common belief was that the Jewish Messiah would liberate the jews from Roman oppresive rule, and restore the kingdom to Israel - Something which Jesus made no attempt to do in his time on earth 2000 years ago.

Have you ever wondered why in our Christmas carols, we sing "Joy to the world, the Lord has come, let Earth receive her King". "Hark, the herald angels sing,

Glory to the newborn king"? Christmas carols are full of reminders that Jesus's title is King. King of what though? King of our hearts, many would say. King of heaven many would say. Could it be that Jesus will one day be King over the earth?

When Herod asked for information from the scribes about the jewish messiah, they said:

'But you, Bethlehem, *in* the land of Judah,
Are not the least among the rulers of Judah;
For out of you shall come a Ruler
Who will shepherd My people Israel.'

But this idea of a king seems to get lost during the gospel story: Yes, throughout Jesus's life, we hear talk about the kingdom of heaven, but no mention of an earthly kingdom. Jesus himself preached "repent for the kingdom of heaven is at hand". The obvious meaning was that this kingdom was not earthly but heavenly. Jesus never called for rebellion against Rome or the jewish leaders. Furthermore, Jesus never referred to himself as an earthly king. So what about all the prophecies of Jesus taking the throne of David, what about Gabriel's message to Mary - How could these promises of God ever come to pass literally?

1 John 3 vs 8 says that the Son of God was revealed to destroy the works of the devil. It says nothing about a plan to establish an earthly kingdom. Furthermore Jesus never claimed to be a king during His time on

Earth. In fact when Jesus asked Peter "who do you say that I am?", Peter said "You are the Messiah, the Son of the living God". And Jesus confirmed his answer was revealed from God. No mention of King of Israel. Even when Jesus was prophesying about the end times in Matthew 24, He calls Himself the Son of Man. "They shall see the Son of Man coming in the clouds".

It is only when Jesus rides into Jerusalem on a donkey, that the crowd start shouting in John 12 vs 13: "Hosanna! Blessed is the **King of Israel** that comes in the name of the Lord". The first time in Jesus's adult life that He is referred to as a king! How did the crowds of Jerusalem arrive at this? Were they busy studying the minor prophets, to know that Zecahriah 9 vs 9 says "fear not, daughter of Zion, Look! Your King comes to you, righteous and victorious, humble and riding on a donkey, on a colt, the foal of a donkey." I honestly do not think so. I believe it was sheer fulfilment of this prophecy by the Spirit of God.

But crowds chanting about the king of Israel caught the attention of Roman governors, and when Jesus was arrested and taken to Pilate, his first question to Jesus in John 18 vs33 was "Are you the King of the Jews?" The reply from Jesus could be translated in modern times to "Huh? You what?" Obviously this was not Jesus's mission 2000 years ago. When pilate pressed Jesus again in verse 37, Jesus replied "it is you who say I am a king. For this sole purpose I was born: to bear witness to the truth." Jesus himself completely shrugged off any claim to be a king. He knew it was not the time to talk about an earthly kingdom. He had a more pressing appointment: To defeat the forces of satan and hell, and to pay the price for the sin of mankind.

And yet when Jesus was nailed to the cross, Pilate wrote a sign and had it put on His cross. The sign read: "JESUS OF NAZARETH THE KING OF THE JEWS". Whether pilate's motive was to mock, or maybe to honour in some small way, it was an act of God. One more tiny reminder that the promise given to Mary 33 years previously had not been forgotten. Even though Jesus had made no mention whatsoever during his ministry about being a king, God had said from the beginning that Jesus would sit on the throne of David, and reign over Israel forever. And once more, God was reminding us all that He will not abandon His promises.

When Jesus lived on earth 2000 years ago, He was not given the throne of David. He did not reign over the house of Jacob, and yes, while His spiritual kingdom is eternal, Jesus had no earthly kingdom. Mary may not have understood as she watched her son being crucified, how this word could ever be fulfilled.

But God had a bigger plan, and if we take these scriptures literally, they tell us that Jesus will one day be given the throne of His father David, and He will reign over the house of Jacob forever. It's in the old testament, and it's in the new: Jesus will rule over Israel and the Earth.

Jesus Himself said to the disciples in Matthew 19 vs 28 "I tell you the truth: In the age when all things are renewed, when the Son of Man sits on his glorious throne, you who have followed me will also sit on 12 thrones, judging the 12 tribes of Israel."

Which throne is this? A heavenly throne, or the throne of David? If it was the heaven ly throne, why would the main objective be to judge (after judgement day is there more judgement?) and why is the focus on the 12 tribes of Israel if this statement refers to Heaven?

Revelation 5 vs 9-10 describes the song sung by the 24 elders:

"You are worthy to take the scroll,
And to open its seals;
For You were slain,
And have redeemed us to God by Your blood
Out of every tribe and tongue and people and nation,
10 And have made us kings and priests to our God;
And **we shall reign** on the earth."

So easy to miss that little detail in verse 10, but it is there! Can we take it literally or is it poetic licence? I am not an expert on theology, but it seems to me that theologians have spent hundreds of years growing symbolic interpretations for parts of scripture that are just honestly too wonderful to comprehend. But in doing so the meaning of scripture is diluted until we lose sight of the real meaning. The elders' song tell us that they will return with Jesus to rule the earth. Can you imagine the 12 disciples, and 12 representatives of the tribes of Israel back here on Earth?

Also this has really struck me: The heavenly elders have only a brief focus on the stage of John's Revelation, but during that song, they firstly praise God for redeeming them, and then they almost cannot contain their excitement, like little chidren, they blurt out, "and we shall reign on earth". I wonder, if the physical Millenium reign of Jesus is not so, why are the heavenly elders so excited about it? Why did they mention this reign on earth? Could it be that they are looking forward to this time? Could the Millenium maybe be a thousand times better than any other period that earth has known?

Even in the Lord's prayer, We recite "Your kingdom come, Your will be done in earth, as it is in Heaven" without realizing that Jesus was even then looking forward to a time that the kingdom of God would be physically ruling on earth. All the way from the beginning to the end of the Bible, there is continual mention of Jesus ruling over the Earth.

When you Put all these scriptures together, all the way from Numbers to Psalms ... to Isaiah and the minor prophets .... to the events of Jesus own 33 years on earth, it is actually impossible to ignore all these pointers towards the belief that Jesus is returning to rule over Israel and the Earth.

5 – Who will be present in the Millenium?

Ok, so far we have established that the Millenium is not a fairy tale, but rather well evidenced if you take scriptures in the old and new testament literally, and in that case, it has to take place to fulfill all the prophecies about Jesus's earthly rule from the Throne of David. Now if this age is almost upon us, the next question has got to be: Who will be here on earth during this age?

The remnant of Jerusalem

We know that when the antichrist invades Jerusalem, there is evidence that half of Israel will escape to the desert. Jesus himself said in Matthew 24 vs 15

"Therefore when you see the 'abomination of desolation,' spoken of by Daniel the prophet, standing in the holy place" (whoever reads, let him understand), **16** "then let those who are in Judea flee to the mountains.

Another scripture that describes this escape to the desert is found in Revelation chapter 12 vs 13-14

13 Now when the dragon saw that he had been cast to the earth, he persecuted the woman who gave birth to the male *Child.* **14** But the woman was given two wings of a great eagle, that she might fly into the wilderness to her place, where she is nourished for a time and times and half a time, from the presence of the serpent. **15** So the serpent spewed water out of his mouth like a flood after the woman, that he might cause her to be carried away by the flood. **16** But the earth helped the woman, and the earth opened its mouth and swallowed up the flood which the dragon had spewed out of his mouth.

Notice that the woman (understood to be Israel) is nourished in the desert for a time, times and half a time. Earlier in the same chapter, it gives a more explicit version of this story: In verse 6, it says: "And the woman fled into the wilderness, where she had a place prepared of God, that they should feed her there a thousand two hundred and three score days. Verse 14 is simply a re-telling of verse 6. The Israelis who flee as Jesus advised will be in the desert for 1260 days. That is 3.5 years if you take a year as 360 days. This means that these Israelis will be alive in the desert at the return of Jesus, and a sensible conclusion is that they will enter the Millenium.

The remnant of the nations who attack Israel in the battle of Armageddon

There will be people of the surrounding enemy nations who are not directly involved in the battle of Armageddon, and so survive at Jesus's return. They will take part in annual feasts, see Zechariah 14 vs 16:

"And it shall come to pass *that* everyone who is left of

all the nations which came against Jerusalem shall go up from year to year to worship the King."

I believe these are the remnant of the arab population of the countries surrounding Israel who were not directly supportive of, or involved in the antichrist system.

The remnant of the Rest of the World

From our background study, we understand that the population of the world will be decimated, a rough estimate is 1 billion remaining at the end of the tribulation, but it could be a lot less. Whatever the numbers, these people will find themselves entering the Millenium. Who most likely would these people be? Most likely the poor and rural populations of Asia, Africa and South America. The third world. I don't believe these are christians (who are raptured at the return of Jesus), but their subsistence lifestyle means that they were not living under the power of the antichrist, and had no reason or desire to take his mark.

Next come those who will be present in the Millenium with immortal or glorified bodies. They will be people who have either gone to heaven already, or were raptured at Jesus's return.

The saints of old

This will be a who's who of the bible: Enoch, Noah, Abraham, Jacob, Joseph, Moses, Joshua, King David, the prophets, the disciples of Jesus, the apostles of the early church and Paul, to name a tiny subset of those who will return with Jesus. This will also include all christians who died in faith over the last 2000 years, well known saints like Smith Wigglesworth, and complete unknowns. Paul speaks of this in 1 Thessalonians 4 vs 14 which says:

For if we believe that Jesus died and rose again, even so God will bring with Him those who sleep in Jesus.

The Martyrs

During the Tribulation Period, it is no secret that many christians will be martyred for their faith. In Revelation chapter 7 vs 14, John is told that the saints he sees before the throne are "those who came out of the great tribulation". And then at the return of Jesus, John says:

4 And I saw thrones, and they sat on them, and judgment was committed to them. Then *I saw* the souls of those who had been beheaded for their witness to Jesus and for the word of God, who had not worshiped the beast or his image, and had not received *his* mark on their foreheads or on their hands. And they lived and reigned with Christ for a thousand years.

The Raptured Church:

Some of the church will survive the Tribulation Period, and these will be raptured at the return of Jesus. Paul says in 1 Thessalonians 4 vs 16-17:

For the Lord Himself will descend from heaven with a shout, with the voice of an archangel, and with the trumpet of God. And the dead in Christ will rise first. **17** Then we who are alive *and* remain shall be caught up together with them in the clouds to meet the Lord in the air. And thus we shall always be with the Lord.

6 - What will happen in the Millenium?

Satan is locked up for the whole 1000 years

Verse 1 of Revelation chapter 20 says:

Then I saw an angel coming down from heaven with the key to the bottomless pit and a heavy chain in his hand. [2] He seized the dragon—that old serpent, who is the devil, Satan—and bound him in chains for a thousand years. [3] The angel threw him into the bottomless pit, which he then shut and locked so Satan could not deceive the nations anymore until the thousand years were finished. Afterward he must be released for a little while.

We are so used to living side by side with evil that I don't think we realize how completely different it will be without satan on this earth. Satan is the mouthpiece that inspires fear and anxiety and paranoia. He sows seeds of regret and self pity that grow into thick bushes of depression, he repeats the sins of others in your memory to make sure that unforgiveness and bitterness and selfishness are normal.

Satan is the driving force behind addictions and greed, temptations and sin. All sexual immorality, pornography, alcohol and drug addictions are pathways that satan pushes people down, until they find too late that the path is slippery, and the destination is hell and destruction.

Satan is the inventor of witchcraft and all false religions, because he loves to give people a faith system which might parallel christianity but it leads to satan instead of God. He loves to deceive. He loves to get close to those jewels of creation that were made to walk with God. He loves to steal God's children.

When people commit murder, you often read that they heard voices telling them to commit these acts. I wonder whose voice that would be? Funny how the world has not figured that out yet?

Many times that Jesus healed the sick, He told an evil spirit to leave the person. It would really be interesting to know just how many diseases are a direct result of an evil spirit.

But now can you imagine a world where all of these influences are absent. For the first time, people of the world will be able to think clearly, objectively and compassionately, without fear. Addictions will have no appeal because their outcomes will always be plain to see. There will be no deceptive faith systems which take you away from God. Heinous crime will be a thing of the past, and so will sickness. I am sure that I am only scratching the surface, but how liberating will it be to live completely free from the oppression of the devil.... I don't think we realize what an absolute change will come about once satan is imprisoned for those thousand years.

Does this mean that there will be no sin during this time? My belief is that the people who survive the tribulation will not be instantly converted. They will still have a sin nature. They will still need grace to be saved, and that saviour will still be Jesus Christ, the Son of God. The only difference is that He will then be living on earth as a king!

Jesus will physically be present for 1000 years, and then for Eternity.

Verse 6 of Revelation chapter 20 says: "... they will be priests of God and of Christ and will reign with Him a thousand years."

Not much else is mentioned of this millenium period in the book of Revelation. All the detail of the wonder of this reign is found in the prophets of the Old Testament. But we can make some assumptions. Since Jesus is the same, yesterday, today and forever, we know that He will have the same authority, the same power and the same compassion that He demonstrated when He walked the land of Israel 2000 years ago.

However there is one difference. Back then, many believed that he was just a carpenter's son. Yes, some followed Him and received from Him, but the general story was one of rejection. John chapter 1 says "He came to His own, and His own did not receive Him. This time He will come as a King. He will be in charge!

One can imagine that in human nature, there might be the temptation to take up this royal role with some vindication in mind. After all the first time round, Jesus was rejected. In many eyes he was a nobody. A trouble maker even. Now imagine this same Jesus returning to this same world, but this time as the king of kings. Do we need to fear that there will be a hidden agenda, to set the records straight? No, a thousand times no! Our saviour has no pride, He carries no offence, He is not returning for His own glory, but for God's. As He said the first time: "I come to do my father's will." He and the Father are one.

This the totally exciting thing. When the one in charge is holy and compassionate, full of wisdom and faith, and the very definition of humility, when Jesus is in charge, one thing is for sure: Rules will be fair and just. Peace will reign, and life can only be a thousand times better than we know it now.

For the first time in the history of this fallen world, there will be total peace, an absence or war.

Isaiah 2 vs 4 and Micah 4 vs 3 says that under the reign of Jesus, nation shall no longer lift up their swords against each other. In fact they will beat their weapons into agricultural tools. Even if that is metaphorical, the implication is that a country's military budget will be used on agriculture. Finally it says that nations will no longer even learn war anymore. To me that speaks of the total absence of armies and political conflict. No need to learn offensive and defensive strategy. For many war-torn countries, it will be a dream come true, and life will instantly be a thousand times better.

Under Jesus reign people will live long, rewarding and content lives.

Isaiah 65 says speaks of the new heavens and the new earth, which we can only compare with the final chapter of Revelation. The following verses speak of this time, but notice that there are sinners present, and some die. We don't believe that sinners will enter the New Jerusalem which comes down from Heaven, and neither will there be death in the New Jerusalem. Therefore what period does this passage describe? Could it be the Millenium?

20 "No more shall an infant from there *live but a few* days,
Nor an old man who has not fulfilled his days;
For the child shall die one hundred years old,
But the sinner *being* one hundred years old shall be accursed.
21 They shall build houses and inhabit *them;*
They shall plant vineyards and eat their fruit.
22 They shall not build and another inhabit;
They shall not plant and another eat;

For as the days of a tree, *so shall be* the days of My people,
And My elect shall long enjoy the work of their hands.
23 They shall not labor in vain,
Nor bring forth children for trouble;
For they *shall be* the descendants of the blessed of the LORD,
And their offspring with them.

As the days of a tree, so shall be the days of my people – I think that says it all. Fig trees live up to 200 years, ashes and beeches live from 300-400 years old, olive trees live over 500 years. The British oak is famed for living up to 1000 years. Yew trees and certain pines live for up to 4000 years.

In verse 20 above, the implication is that something is wrong if you die at 100 in the Millenium. And the emphasis is that people in the Millenium will enjoy the whole spectrum of life's experiences: work, house ownership, children, these will be deeply rewarding, and these rewards will not be taken away, nor will they turn into trouble, but will be richly enjoyed during this time.

Amos 9 from verse 11 also describes the restoration of Israel "on that day". What day is this? Could it be the "Day of the Lord"?

Jesus will teach from the Bible

Just as He did 2000 years ago, Jesus will spend His

days teaching. Is that any surprise? Isaiah chapter 2 vs 4 says:

"He will teach us His ways, And we shall walk in His paths. For out of Zion shall go forth the law, And the word of the LORD from Jerusalem."

When you read the gospels, you see crowds listening to Jesus everywhere He went. How come? Jesus had no public relations board, no advertising campaign. But every time He spoke it says that the people were astonished at His doctrine: For He taught them as one who had authority, and not as the scribes.

Is it any wonder? He is The Word of God. Jesus was with God in the beginning. Jesus was God in the beginning. All things were made by Him. No wonder He has authority. He knows what He is talking about!

2000 years ago, people were so hungry for the words of Jesus that they camped out on a mountain to listen to Him, no food stalls nearby. In this day and age, we have a few good bible teachers, but everything will pale in comparison when Jesus opens His mouth to teach.

The Word of God created the universe. The Word of God has the power to bring itself to pass. The Word of God is life to your body, and healing to your bones. Life is in the Word. I don't think we have a fraction of an idea about the importance of knowing, and feeding on, and daily hearing, and understanding, and obeying the Word of God. Do we have any idea what power is in God's Word?

I do not think we have scratched the dust on the surface of this, we are all deeply in need of being taught by Jesus, the one who spoke, and the worlds were created.

Under Jesus reign, Israel will be the greatest kingdom on Earth

Isaiah chapter 2 vs 2 says: "Now it shall come to pass in the latter days t*hat* the mountain of the LORD's house shall be established on the top of the mountains, and shall be **exalted** above the hills; And all nations shall flow to it."

Micah chapter 4 vs 7 says: "I will make the lame a remnant, and the outcast a strong nation; So the LORD will reign over them in Mount Zion from now on, even forever."

Nahum chapter 2 vs 2 says: "For the Lord will restore the excellence of Jacob"

Zephaniah chapter 3 vs 20 says: "At that time I will bring you back, even at the time I gather you; For I will give you fame and praise among all the peoples of the earth,
When I return your captives before your eyes,"

Zechariah chapter 8 vs 13 says "And it shall come to pass that just as you were a curse among the nations, O house of Judah and house of Israel, so I will save you, and you shall be a blessing. Do not fear, Let your hands be strong.' "

Haggai chapter 2 vs 6-9
"For thus says the LORD of hosts: 'Once more (it *is* a little while) I will shake heaven and earth, the sea and dry land; and I will shake all nations, and they shall come to the Desire of All Nations, and I will fill this temple with glory,' says the LORD of hosts. 'The silver *is* Mine, and the gold *is* Mine,' says the LORD of hosts. 'The glory of this latter temple shall be greater than the former,' says the LORD of hosts. 'And in this place I will give peace,' says the LORD of hosts."

Ezekiel 34 vs 26-27,29 says "I will make them and the places all around My hill a blessing; and I will cause showers to come down in their season; there shall be showers of blessing. Then the trees of the field shall yield their fruit, and the earth shall yield her increase. They shall be safe in their land; I will raise up for them a garden of renown, and they shall no longer be consumed with hunger in the land, nor bear the shame of the Gentiles anymore.

Jesus will reign over His enemies (the nations who have been enemies to Israel), He will judge nations and peoples.

Psalm 2 vs 8 "Ask of me and I will give you the nations for your inheritance, and the ends of the earth for your possession. You shall break them with a rod of iron; you shall dash them to pieces like a potter's vessel."

Notice that Jesus will reign with a rod of iron, inferring that He will have complete control over all laws and all nations.

Before we get into any more scriptures, i sense you recoiling a bit. The Jesus we know from the gospels is the humble servant, the gentle shepherd. The one who let the woman caught in adultery go free. The one who said "let the children come to me". The one who was led like a lamb to the slaughter. The one who gave his life to save us. Has Jesus changed during the last 2000 years into a power-hungry warlord? Not one bit. He is the same. He cannot change. He will always be humble and merciful. However Jesus has never been afraid to confront hypocrites and enemies. Also be careful how you read "reign with a rod of iron". It is easy to interpret this as totalitarian harsh and intrusive government, which takes away your rights, and restricts your freedom (think communism or sharia).

But this is not consistent with the heart of God. Rather, it is more in line with God's heart that under Jesus's reign, each nation will be under instruction to work in perfect harmony with the government of

Jesus. Therefore the national laws set by Jesus will be followed by every nation, to ensure that all life is fair and just. I do not believe this means that personal freedom will be removed, it just means that the laws of each nation will be in complete harmony with the word of God.

Being strict and in total control only translates to harsh if the ruler is harsh. When the ruler is wise and compassionate, it is always beneficial for subjects if the ruler is strict and in total control. It creates a secure atmosphere where everyone knows exactly where they stand, and where no-one gets away with breaking the law. In other words, Jesus will make sure that every criminal is caught, and everyone who pushes against the law of God will receive a fair consequence. It means that laws will be policed fairly. It means that there will be no room in the police forces for beligerent prejudiced officers. In every arena of life there will be professional accountability.

So the iron rod rule of Jesus is not something to be afraid of or repulsed by. Rather it will create a world of peace and security, simply because the ruler is infinitely loving and wise. And where is the proof that Jesus's reign will be loving and wise? Isaiah 16 vs 5 says "A throne will be established in **lovingkindness**, and a judge will sit on it in faithfulness in the tent of David. Moreover He will seek justice, and be prompt in righteousness." Since Isaiah's time no such king has sat on David's throne.

But ... I hear you say ... it says that Jesus will not just rule, but **break** the nations with a rod of iron. If that were not clear enough, it says that He will **dash** them to pieces like a potter's vessel. Where is my Jesus who went looking for the lost sheep, rejoicing over one repentant sinner? Has anger replaced compassion? No! Jesus breaks only to put back together. Where a nation's government is rotten from the ground up, Jesus will have to break down that government, and build it back up the right way. Where a nation needs to be broken into smaller entities, Jesus will break up these nations, and institute government at a more local level. If these nations are what we would call super powers, then yes, the arrival of Jesus and His millenial reign will smash these super powers, so that they feel like a clay pot smashed into pieces. But again I want to emphasize, this will be a good thing. Jesus will not break people, He will break nations where it is necessary.

Jesus will bring justice to the poor

Psalm 72 appears to describe Soloman king of Israel until you get to verse 5 (They shall fear you ... througout all generations), verse 8 (He shall have dominion from sea to sea and from the river to the ends of the Earth), verse 11 (All kings shall fall down before Him, all nations shall serve him), verse 17 (His name shall endure for ever, and men shall be blessed in Him, and all nations shall call Him blessed).

It is at this point that you realize, while parts of this describe Solomon's reign (eg the gold of Sheba given to Him), there is absolutely no way that Solomon is feared forever, nor did he have dominion over the ends of the Earth, nor did all nations serve Him, nor will Solomon's name endure forever. But this psalm perfectly describes the earthly rule of Jesus, the son of David. And one thing it keeps on repeating is that:

He will judge the poor with justice (vs 2),
He will bring justice to the poor of the people, and save the children of the needy, and will break in pieces the oppresor (vs 4)
He will deliver the needy when he cries, the poor also and him who has no helper (vs 12)
He will spare the poor and needy .... and precious shall be their blood in His sight. (vs 13-14)

One thing it does not say, is that Jesus will create a utopia, where there are no poor. There will be poor, but Jesus's rule will prioritise them, give them justice, give their children opportunities to succeed and be saved out of poverty, and most significantly, Jesus will eradicate oppresion and slavery from the earth so that the poor are no longer exploited but supported.

Jesus will build a new temple

A big feature of the Millenium will be a new temple
Isaiah chapter 56 vs 6-7 says

"Everyone who keeps from defiling the Sabbath, And holds fast My covenant, 7 even them I will bring to My holy mountain, and make them joyful in My house of prayer. Their burnt offerings and their sacrifices *will be* accepted on My altar; for My house shall be called a house of prayer for all nations."

Then, if you read Ezekiel chapters 40-48, you will find details of a vision that Ezekiel had concerning a jewish temple. It describes the dimensions, the building details, the priesthood and the sacrifices.

This temple has caused much debate throughout christendom as the Ezekiel account describes burnt offerings which seem to oppose the gospel truth that no further sacrifice is necessary since Christ was our eternal sacrifice. I don't know all the answers, but I do know that God's plans will not dishonour Jesus, and i know that the Word of God will stand forever. Some have explained that the Millenium temple sacrifices will serve as a reminder looking back to the sacrifice of Jesus.

Ezekiel 37 vs 24-28
24 "David My servant *shall be* king over them, and they shall all have one shepherd; they shall also walk in My judgments and observe My statutes, and do them. **25** Then they shall dwell in the land that I have given to Jacob My servant, where your fathers dwelt; and they shall dwell there, they, their children, and their children's children, forever; and My servant David *shall be* their prince forever. **26** Moreover I will

make a covenant of peace with them, and it shall be an everlasting covenant with them; I will establish them and multiply them, and I will set My sanctuary in their midst forevermore. **27** My tabernacle also shall be with them; indeed I will be their God, and they shall be My people. **28** The nations also will know that I, the LORD, sanctify Israel, when My sanctuary is in their midst forevermore.

Safety

Safety will be a hallmark of the Millenium. Children will play in the streets, wild animals will no longer pose a threat to each other, or to mankind. Can you imagine a society where no one has any sinister habits or intentions, so that you never think twice about letting your children play outside in the streets. Isaiah chapter 11 vs 6-9 describes animals living in harmony who would today be hunter and prey. This passage finishes by saying no one, no animal shall hurt or destroy in all of God's holy mountain. This is the depth of change that will come about under Jesus reign. Even the very motives and impulses that today drive carnivores to hunt, will be gone.

It should not be a surprise: When Jesus is present on the Earth, the intensity of God's presence will permeate every living being, so that the value of another's life will be the uttermost thought, even amongst animals. Can you imagine animals acting as if they are full of the Spirit of God? Can you imagine wolves nurturing lambs? Can you imagine foxes playing with squirrels? Can you imagine a cat having no desire to pounce on a robin? There will be harmony between all living things, as has never been witnessed. The animals will tell a story – something has changed. They will all prove that the Millenium reign of Jesus is established in love, and this love is so deep and powerful that even the nature of animals are forever changed.

Such safety willl be enjoyed by all, such harmony, that it is hard to imagine. Today we live in a dog eat dog world where many have been hurt, and so they hurt back. But in the Millenium the presence and love of God will be so strong, the knowledge of God will fill the earth, and so not only people but animals will find it unthinkable to take another's life, we will all truly love our neighbours, life will be precious in everyone's sight. This atmosphere of safety and peace is the subject of Ezekiel 34:

Ezekiel 34 vs 25-30
25 "I will make a covenant of peace with them, and cause wild beasts to cease from the land; and they will dwell safely in the wilderness and sleep in the woods. **26** I will make them and the places all around My hill a blessing; and I will cause showers to come down in their season; there shall be showers of blessing. **27** Then the trees of the field shall yield their fruit, and the earth shall yield her increase. They shall be safe in their land; and they shall know that I *am*

the LORD, when I have broken the bands of their yoke and delivered them from the hand of those who enslaved them. **28** And they shall no longer be a prey for the nations, nor shall beasts of the land devour them; but they shall dwell safely, and no one shall make *them* afraid.

7 - The Millenium and the parables of Jesus

The kingdom of God, or the kingdom of Heaven can mean the people who are under the lordship of Jesus, those who are born of God through faith in God. It can also refer to the physical kingdom that will be manifest during the Millenium. Most "kingdom parables" refer to the spiritual kingdom of God. An example is the parable of the forgiven servant who did not forgive his own debt. This illustrates the importance of forgiveness in the spiritual kingdom of God.

When the rich young ruler went away from Jesus, Jesus's reply was "How hard it is for those with riches to enter the kingdom of God". We don't read this to mean that rich people will find it difficult to enter the Millenium kingdom. We understand that Jesus was referring to the spiritual kingdom, the family of God. On the other hand, some parables really don't make sense unless you understand them to illustrate the Millenium kingdom, and it is these I want to focus on in this chapter.

Matthew 13 vs 31-32 is the mustard seed parable:

31 Another parable He put forth to them, saying: "The kingdom of heaven is like a mustard seed, which a man took and sowed in his field, 32 which indeed is the least of all the seeds; but when it is grown it is

greater than the herbs and becomes a tree, so that the birds of the air come and nest in its branches."

When God sowed this tiny seed of His kingdom, it was indeed the smallest kingdom in the world. In fact it was a family - Abraham's family. and when this famly grew to become a people of two million living in Egypt, one would not think of comparing them to the mighty kingdoms of Egypt or Assyria or Babylon. And after this people under Joshua's leadership established the country of Israel, they were constantly under attack throughout history. You could call them the baby brother of the countries of the Middle East.

Yes God was on their side, and through faith in God, they won some amazing battles. But without God they were nothing. Without God, their size was always evident. They were always the least. Today, not too much has changed. The nation of Israel is back in the land of promise, and while they have won some notable victories (1967), they are still under the gun from Hezbollah and the PLO. They are still obliged to international agreements regarding their borders. Therefore we can see that "when it is grown" has not yet come to pass. They are still the least.

However we know from prophecy that in the Millenium, Israel will be elevated as the greatest country in the world. So it looks like the MIllenium will provide the conclusion for this parable. During this time, Israel will be grown. It will no longer be the least, but instead will be greater than all other kingdoms, so that the birds of the air come and nest in its branches.

A strange end to the parable, for "birds of the air" is used in other parables to describe satan (stealing the seed which fell on the path). We know that satan will be bound during the Millenium, unable to influence and certainly not able to nest in the kingdom of Israel. However we do know that the remnants of the former enemies of Israel will attend the feasts and travel to Jerusalem, where they will be taught by Jesus, and will therefore have the chance to begin again. In that sense, the remnant of the former enemies of Israel will come to Israel to find spiritual shelter, spiritual food and a spiritual home. Maybe even to set up homes and take on citizenship.

Matthew 13 vs 33 is the leaven parable:

[33] Another parable He spoke to them: "The kingdom of heaven is like leaven, which a woman took and hid in three measures of meal till it was all leavened.

What is leaven? It is simply fermenting dough which under the right conditions, releases carbon dioxide and therefore when it is mixed with bread dough, causes the bread dough to rise and expand, as it creates many air pockets in the bread dough. In the bible, leaven is mentioned mainly in the context of sin. Jesus said "Beware the leaven of pharisees". Paul said in reference to removing an unrepentant sinner from the church "Do you not know that a little leaven leavens the whole lump of dough?". In other words, leaven spreads virally. It keeps on spreading until the whole environment is affected. But now we hear leaven being used in a positive context. Here, Jesus says that the kingdom of Heaven is like leaven. Why three measures of meal? Could this represent the approximate 2000 years since Jesus died (and the promise of the kingdom became available to everyone) plus the 1000 years of the MIllenium during which the leaven of His word and Spirit will permeate the whole world, so that it really can be said that the knowledge of God will fill the earth as the waters cover the sea?

Luke 19 vs 11-27 is the parable of the minas (a coin during Jesus first time on earth)

Now as they heard these things, He spoke another parable, because He was near Jerusalem and because they thought the kingdom of God would appear immediately. Therefore He said: "A certain nobleman went into a far country to receive for himself a kingdom and to return. So he called ten of his servants, delivered to them ten minas, and said to them, 'Do business till I come.' But his citizens hated him, and sent a delegation after him, saying, 'We will not have this *man* to reign over us.'

"And so it was that when he returned, having received the kingdom, he then commanded these servants, to whom he had given the money, to be called to him, that he might know how much every man had gained by trading. Then came the first, saying, 'Master, your mina has earned ten minas.' And he said to him, 'Well *done,* good servant; because you were faithful in a very little, have authority over ten cities.' And the second came, saying, 'Master, your mina has earned five minas.' Likewise he said to him, 'You also be over five cities.'

"Then another came, saying, 'Master, here is your mina, which I have kept put away in a handkerchief. For I feared you, because you are an austere man. You collect what you did not deposit, and reap what you did not sow.' And he said to him, 'Out of your own mouth I will judge you, *you* wicked servant. You knew that I was an austere man, collecting what I did not deposit and reaping what I did not sow. Why then did you not put my money in the bank, that at my coming I might have collected it with interest?'

"And he said to those who stood by, 'Take the mina from him, and give *it* to him who has ten minas.' (But they said to him, 'Master, he has ten minas.') 'For I say to you, that to everyone who has will be given; and from him who does not have, even what he has will be taken away from him. But bring here those enemies of mine, who did not want me to reign over them, and slay *them* before me.' "

The interesting thing about this parable is that the bible explains why it was told: Jesus was getting near Jerusalem, and the people thought that He was about to take over as king, and begin to reign. So in order to put His physical reign over Jerusalem into perspective, He told this parable to illustrate that:

1. Before Jesus is given the kingdom of Israel, He has to go far away and then return.
2. As He leaves, Jesus distributes gifts to his servants, and instructs them to do business till he returns.
3. His citizens (not the servants) then rebel and make it clear they do not want Him to be king.
4. When Jesus returns he demands an account of his investment from His servants.
5. The servant's faithfulness in carrying out instructions is rewarded by authority over cities.
6. The servant who did not invest his mina was harshly condemned. Apparently he could have obeyed in some small way (eg invest in the bank) but even this he did not do, probably for fear of losing the mina, since he was afraid of his master.
7. Jesus then judged the rebel citizens with death.

What does this all mean?

Firstly, the establishment of this kingdom is a future event, and will not happen until Jesus has returned from a far place. Secondly, what are the minas? Could they represent literal money? Is this a parable about financial stewardship? I think the answer lies in Acts chapter 1 vs 8 where Jesus said "you will receive power when the Holy Spirit comes on you", and also in John chapter 16 vs 7: where Jesus says "unless I go away, the Holy Spirit will not come to you". So there is one gift which Jesus gave his children at his departure, it was the deposit of the Holy Spirit.

What about Jesus's instruction "do business till I return". What can that mean when applied to a gift which is not monetary, but spiritual? Again, the bible tells the story, for we only need to look at Jesus final instructions to his disciples. The business that Jesus referred to is summed up in these final words in Mark 16 vs 15; "Go into all the world, and **preach** the gospel to every creature". For those who really like to see the illustration in complete detail, think of this: As you do business by investing money in good projects, the invested money multiplies and you end up with much more than your initial investment. Similarly when you use the gift of the Holy Spirit to preach and witness, you multiply that gift, because the hearers will believe and receive , and you end up with more gift bearing believers than you started with.

And what of the reward? Strangely this can be taken more literally. In more than one place Jesus tells his disciples that they will rule with him in the future.

Matthew 19 vs 28

Jesus said to them, "I assure you *and* most solemnly say to you, in the renewal [that is, the Messianic restoration and regeneration of all things] when the Son of Man sits on His glorious throne, you [who have followed Me, becoming My disciples] will also sit on twelve thrones, judging the twelve tribes of Israel.

Similarly in 1 Corinthians 6, Paul says that the saints will judge the world. In two places in Revelation, there is mention of the saints ruling: chapter 5 vs 10: "He has made us kings and priests unto our God, and we shall reign on the earth." And chapter 21 vs 6 says: "Blessed and holy is he that has part in the first resurrection, on such the second death has no power, but they shall be priests of God and of Christ, and shall reign with Him a thousand years."

At first sight this reward does not seem to hold much attraction. Typically leadership is synonomous with pressure, public unpopularity, huge responsibility, public mistakes and the list goes on. Few of us are born to be leaders, most of us are content to follow. But there is one difference, this saintly leadership will take place in the Millenium. Jesus will not lead a government which creates stress and grief for His saints. It will be a joy, it will be amazing to work in Jesus's government. For one thing, this reward means returning to live in the Millenium, which will be simply a thousand times better than anything you have experienced on earth. Life will be rich, full, diverse, rewarding, and you will be working hand in hand with King Jesus!

So does this mean that the more people you have converted to Christ, the higher up the Millenium government you will sit? Not quite. Monetary profit is simple. If your pound has made £100 , then it is simple success. If you have converted 100 people to Christ, I believe that there is more in the balance than numbers.

In other words, has the conviction of your speech so stirred up the hearers heart, that they are forever changed? Has the holiness of your life so impressed the hearer that they are humbled forever to follow your Lord? Has the power evident in your life so affected the hearer that they cannot deny the love of God? I believe that the result of Jesus's deposit of the Holy Spirit in our lives will be a combination of all these, and upon the depth of these combined results, our obedience will be accounted.

And because we can all fake sincerity, holiness and power, the actual measuring stick will be: how much did we realize that we are nothing without God, how much did we pray, how much did we feed on God's word, knowing that our lives and our faith would be dead without connecting to the vine? And finally how much did we follow through and put ourselves on the line to stand up for Jesus? Now you can see why Jesus said:

[21] "Not everyone who says to Me, 'Lord, Lord,' shall enter the kingdom of heaven, but he who does the will of My Father in heaven. [22] Many will say to Me in that day, 'Lord, Lord, have we not prophesied in Your name, cast out demons in Your name, and done many wonders in Your name?' [23] And then I will declare to them, 'I never knew you; depart from Me, you who practice lawlessness!'

I have often wondered how this could ever be possible. But imagine: You get into professional ministry, and you can get into the place where you are minstering in your own strength, where you are proud of your position, your church, your particular role. To the point where you have big numbers (church members) but as there is little depth to your life, there is little depth to your converts. To the point where you have got supernatural God-given gifts (which God gives for the benefit of the hearer, not to make you look good by the way!) but you have left behind the intimacy of the relationship with your saviour and God, and now you find that you are a stranger to the heart of God.

Which brings us to the servant (notice he was still a servant, not a rebellious citizen) who did not go about his lord's business. Yes he might have numbers which look like there was a return on the deposit of the Holy Spirit. But it was all human effort. Or maybe he was a believer who was called to ministry, but decided to keep things nice and safe, by ignoring the call.

Whatever the scenario, the servant who did not go about his Lord's business lost it all. We don't know quite what that means, but it would be good to make a decision never to find out. So if you feel like the servant with the mina safely wrapped up, now is the time to do at least the bare minimum, use the Holy Spirit's gift in some way, but use it with prayer and faith. Don't rely on your own talent, don't measure by worldly success, stay close to God, and witness for Him! The main thing to get from this parable is that the top priority for those who want to be part of the Millenium Kingdom, is to make yourself available to God to be used for His Glory.

8 - How will the MIllenium work - my thoughts

Salvation

This is a strange one. With Jesus sat on a throne in Israel, why will people need faith anymore? The Saviour and Messiah will be there reigning in Israel for all to see. Surely faith is what we place in an invisible God, it is the substance of things not seen, so how will people be saved in the Millenium? By repentance and faith in Jesus, the same as now. And the survivors of the Tribulation Period will be ripe for salvation.

As the Millenium progresses, many children will be born to the remnant of Israel, the remnant of the enemy nations, and the remnant of the Earth's population. These children will have never seen Jesus's return. They never witnessed being spared horrible death in the tribulation. These children will need faith to believe that the one sitting on the throne is who He says He is. That He is the Son of God. That He has descended from heaven. And salvation will come as it does now. Through repentance and acceptance of Jesus as Lord. Through God's grace, and through faith in Jesus.

Money/Economy

During the reign of Jesus, we have seen that Israel and the nations who submit to His reign will experience abundance. The economy will not be a struggle and a battle, it will no longer be driven by fear or greed. The curse which applied to Adam (reaping from the ground by the sweat of his brow) and which has affected us all since Adam's time, will no longer apply. Success and abundance will come naturally.

No longer will money be worshipped, no longer will the rich exploit the poor, instead Jesus will make sure that the poor are helped. There will be a wealth transfer to Israel. Jesus will use this wealth to bring justice to the poor. I don't believe that debt will exist. The poor will be greatly helped, and will not need the curse of debt to buy what they need. Since the economy will be controlled by one who is all loving and all wise, He will not be interested in making gain from lending money. Jesus will not exploit the needs of people, instead His reign will supply needs.

Think about the astronomical price of property these days. It has become the biggest burden in our budgets, and causes untold stress and debt. Why have property prices quadrupled in the last 20 years? Who is the money going to? Not to the seller, he simply uses the money to buy his next house in most cases. The money goes to the bank, it's simply more cash for them to invest in their game of investment. We are supplying the funds with which banks play their money games. Except that it's no game because as property prices go up, it causes stress, family breakdown and debt. And it will certainly be no game when banks go under.

I don't believe that Jesus will play these games. His reign will transform the economy, Isaiah 65 vs 21 says that people will build houses and live in them, they shall not build and another occupy. And i don't believe that people will have to borrow to pay for a house to be built. Land could be free, or at least at a price the poor can afford.

Finally will there be a welfare system? I really cannot see our wise King resorting to systems that we invented in the twentieth century, and which are far from perfect, and even create their own new problems. It is much more believeable to think that Jesus will (as part of His care of the poor throughout the world) resource the education and development of all poor so that they all find their destiny. With no system to abuse, the poor will receive the future that they really need. Jesus will give dignity, ability, vision and hope to every poor person who lives in the Millenium, I believe.

Technology and Media

There is no reason to believe that the technological advancement of the human race will suddenly disappear in the new age. Even if all cities are completely destroyed in the final earthquake, mankind should be able to quickly rebuild technology that will be used in the Millenium. Just as today, technology will allow businesses to expand and information and media to be published. However i cannot believe that Jesus will allow anything vain or evil to be supported by technology. Technology will only exist to support what is good in God's sight. And it could be that instead of technology playing a pervasive part in society, as it does today, it's role may be diminished, and only serve certain basic needs to optimize efficiencies in society.

Sport

Will there be sport in the Millenium? I think so, at a very grass roots and enjoyable level, and the key will probably be participation, not watching. The main thing to take away, is that mankind will just have been through such horror that they will not, they can not, return to vain pursuits and the emptyness of success, fame, fortune, mindless entertainment and self indulgence. Instead life will be deeply purposeful, rewarding and enjoyable.

Entertainment

Will there be music and art in the Millenium? I believe so, as these are simply reflections of the beauty of Heaven. Where I think the line will be drawn, is that nothing will be done in vain pursuit. Today, much of music and art glorifies evil, or at the very least, man and his base desires. In the Millenium I can only think that art and music will have one purpose and inspiration: to capture people's hearts for God. But why, you may ask, with Jesus ruling the world, will people need any further expression of God's nature? Why then in heaven do we have musical instruments? Why do the angels worship God in song? Is not His presence enough? God in His wisdom invented music and art as mediums through which we could express our love for Him, and and which communicate the beauty of God. And so it will be, I believe, in the MIllenium.

So you could not really call it entertainment, for entertainment's sake. But there will surely be a culmination of art forms in the Millenium which reflect the love of people for their Saviour and King.

It goes without saying that all forms of recreation under the label of vices (think gambling, recreational drugs, pornography, X rated films amongst others) will be absent from the MIllenium in my humble view. Those who fed on these vices in the past may mourn their passing, but will soon be relieved when they find that they are finally free.

Culture

Will there be cultural diversity in the MIllenium, or will the human race look like a ramshackle remnant of survivors, bereft of any souvenirs of their culture or past? I cannot see it in God's heart to somehow take away the identity of the survivors of the Tribulation Period, so that everyone takes on one culture.

I see it in God's heart to allow survivors from every part of the world to richly express their culture, simply because one hallmark of God's creation is uniqueness and individuality. There will be no grey area where it comes to religions, however. Followers of false religions will just have seen the absolute poverty of their beliefs to save them from the events of the tribulation.

They will all know that it is by God's grace that they are alive. They will all know that Jesus is His son, and that He reigns! However i don't believe that the absence of other religions will detract from the cultural diversity that will be richly experienced during the Millenium. The food, customs, dress, practices and strengths of a culture will remain, the deception of false religions will be removed.

Education

Will children go to school in the Millenium? I am sure they will, or at least, as in old times, they will learn a trade from their family. Under Jesus's reign, I cannot see education being presented as the precursor to money driven careers. Children will need to learn as they do today, but I believe that in the Millenium, education will help a child develop his or her gifting, so that individual goals are realised without the entry into what we call the rat race. That, i believe, will be part of the beauty of living under the reign of Jesus. People will develop into their God-given purpose. No more "i wish i had done this or that". Under Jesus's wisdom, all people will reach fulfilling destinies. It sounds too good to be true, that not a single life will follow the treadmill of boredom and monotony at work. But that is why I have entitled this book "One thousand times better". I cannot see how the physical presence of Jesus on our Earth could result in anything less than creative, exciting, purposeful, fulfilled and beautiful lives, for the poor, the rich and everyone in between.

Legal system

With Jesus as the King of kings, and the Judge of judges, you can expect a completely fair and righteous legal system. The days of lawyers winning a case purely by the virtue of their flair for excellent case argument ... are gone. No longer will there be any miscarriage of justice. Where someone is guilty, they will face the relevant penalty. Where someone is innocent, they will not be convicted. The days of ignoring compelling evidence in court, and overturning an evidenced prosecution by clever argument ... are gone. And similarly, the days of convicting the wrong man, while the guilty go free ... are gone.

Healthcare

There is so much mention of divine health and healing in passages that refer to the Millenium, that one does wonder, will we need a healthcare system in this period? Maybe, but I believe that anyone who is sick will firstly come to Jesus for healing.

Transport and utilities
Will there be roads and cars? Will there be trains and planes? Will we need gas and electricity? Will we need telephones? Will we still have water mains supply? It is possible to go a bit mad about the Millenium period, and imagine that people will suddenly acquire supernatural abilities to communicate and travel without the infrastructure that now exists. Yes those of us with glorified bodies may be able to transcend the laws of nature, but the rest of the population of the world will benefit from all the mod cons that we now enjoy.

Church

Now to **the** question: Will there be church in the Millenium? Are you kidding? There will be church like you have never seen in your life! One thing we know about Heaven - there is continual worship at the throne of God. I am talking about angelic, orchestral, beautiful worship. And Jesus prayed: "your kingdom come, your will be done on earth, as it is in heaven" Do you think for one moment that Jesus is going to back out of that?

My friend, in the Millenium there is going to be church like nothing else. There will be no need for different buildings, denominations or congregations, for Jesus will be our high Priest, our teacher and our pastor, and we His flock will worship at His throne. Gone will be the days of the eldership taking over, gone will be the days of the pastor fleecing his flock, gone will be the days of man made traditions.

Will there be sermons? Yes. The same Jesus who preached the sermon on the mount, will preach again and again. Will there be spontaneous worship songs? Yes! The same Jesus who said "if they stop praising me, the very rocks will cry out" will receive our heartfelt and authentic praise. Will there be a choir of angels? Why not? And add to that a drumset, bass guitar, piano, guitar and whole orchestra...

But you may ask - We will all be saved saints living in glorified bodies, and satan will not even feature on earth. What need will there be for victory and spiritual warfare? Apart from worshipping Jesus and working in His government, I believe we will spend the Millenium preaching to and teaching the tribulation survivors, interceding for their precious souls, and seeing many saved. We also know that Jesus will have a world wide mission to help the poor, and every saint will be involved. You will find treasures among those poor country folk. We certainly don't need to worry about whether the

Millenium church will have purpose. King Jesus will ensure that!

9 - Conclusion and What now?

In this day and age of technology and advance, we live in a society that for the most part has reasoned God out of their lives. It is almost sheer stupidity in most educated folks ears, to suggest that the creator of this universe is going to appear once again as God the Son, but this time instead of being born in a stable, He will appear with armies, defeat the antichrist, throw satan into a pit and take charge of the earth.

And yet we can accept that Jesus lived on earth 2000 years ago and had authority over the devil wherever he went. Surely, given the example set the first time, it is not too much of a stretch to believe that prophecy will be fulfilled this time around too.

The almost unbelievable thing is that this Millenium period is on the horizon. Once the antichrist begins his beastly rule, we have a very short period until Jesus returns and the beginning of the Millenium. In the light of this, can you see the dangerous deception of following beliefs like amillenialism (which teaches that there will be no millennial reign on earth) or postmillenialism (which teaches that we are already living in the Millenium).

Neither of these theories help the christian to have a sense of urgency, or a sense of preparation to be part of this period. In fact the symbolism of amillenialism and the familiarity of postmillenialism can only serve to lull the christian deeper into sleep, because according to these theories, it will either not actually take place, or it is the life that we already know. And therefore there is no anticipation. There is no wake up call. There is no taking the bible literally. There is confusion as to when you can take God literally. Friends, these are deceptions that we cannot afford as we get closer to the time of the antichrist. For this very reason i believe that it is of utmost importance to have a biblical understanding of the nature and the reality of the soon coming Millenium.

What now? I want you to imagine that you are back at school, and the teacher has just set a horrible maths test, that even the mathematicians hate. It is literally the closest thing to hell that you can imagine. Then the teacher is called out of the classroom. What now? you would soon start chatting ... playing ... fighting maybe even. Then you hear "TEACHER'S COMING!!!!". When the alarm sounds, there are two things that happen to this class:

Firstly they stop misbehaving. Not one child says to himself "Now that is just hypocritical ... I was throwing a book a minute ago, I should really just keep on throwing books around so that my teacher can see exactly what a fool I am". The thought does not cross one mind. No! The fear of God comes on every child and makes all classroom misbehaving repulsive to even consider. This is exactly the result we need as we hear prophets call out the hour we are living in. People only sin when they think they can get away with it. We need to see end time prophets as a blessing, a much needed alarm which bring us to our senses, and cause all spiritual senses to sharpen, making sin a repulsion.

Secondly these children start getting on with what the teacher asked when they left the room. Suddenly the mind focusses ... an interest develops for the instructions left by the teacher. How amazing! Suddenly, completing the maths assignment becomes more interesting than winning a rubber band paper flicking war!

And so it is for us. If the Millenium is close, how much closer is the Tribulation Period? How much more should we put our lives and prayer into winning souls. But God is so good. His return is framed not only with warning for those who are asleep spiritually, but also with the amazing promise of the Millenium for those who wake up spiritually.

So back to the classroom for one minute. In his wisdom and with an open show of generosity, our teacher has promised that all children who complete the torturous maths test will be treated, not just for an afternoon, but to Disneyland Florida for a month's holiday in America. I don't need to explain how that promise will help these children focus, how it will help them endure the awful torture, how it will enable them to persevere and not give up.

Many people have wondered about the purpose of the Millenium. Could it just be that Jesus knew that the church needed a hope and a goal to keep focussed on during the awful tribulation that is around the corner? That, like the teacher in our story, Jesus knows that without an outlandish reward many will be led astray, many will lose heart, many will turn their backs on the faith.

God is so good, when you look at the big picture, He has planned a reward which is the exact opposite of the tribulation. That is one reason why it is such a travesty of biblical teaching to say that the reign of Jesus in the MIllenium is not really going to happen on earth, or that perhaps we are already living in the Millenium. Let's not be like a stupid child, who cannot even bring himself to believe the generosity of their parent's reward, and so carries on misbehaving. My prayer is that the knowledge of the Millenium, and Jesus's physical reign on earth will keep you on track when end times cause many to fail and give up. Amen?

Printed in Great Britain
by Amazon

39276263R00056